THE
"NEVER BETTER"
CLUB

Michael McCaffrey

A publication of

Eber & Wein Publishing

Pennsylvania

The "Never Better" Club

Copyright © 1997, 2015 by Michael McCaffrey

First edition published 1997. Second edition 2015

Library of Congress
Cataloging in Publication Data

ISBN 978-1-60880-466-5

Proudly manufactured in the United States of America
by

Eber & Wein Publishing
Pennsylvania

Author's Thoughts

This book is not just about my father, but about his wonderful outlook on life, to describe him as an optimist would be an understatement. Day or night, if anyone asked him how he was doing, he would always respond, "Never better." Most of us are realists. When we are asked how we are doing, we answer with an OK, or good, or sometimes just plain awful. So how can it be that a person could ignore realism, and live in a seemingly perfect "never better" world? As I grew up I asked myself this question, over and over again, as I listened to my father's philosophy. After going through a series of dramatic changes in my life, I was finally won over by my dad's views. I had become a member of the "Never Better" Club so to speak.

My dad always pointed out that the club has no dues and no meetings. The only commitment to be a member of the club is to be "never better," twenty-four hours a day, seven days a week. It's all in the attitude! It is my sincere hope that everyone that reads this book will become a member of the club. There may be drugs we can take to forget disappointments, therapists we can pay to cure us, and priests we can summon to chase away the demons, but inside each one of us is our own voice telling us we can accomplish all we want from within.

Choose to be "never better."

"Our Lord, Jesus Christ, started the 'Never Better Club' when he said, 'Rejoice always!'"

"Ordinary people doing extraordinary things."

"The secret of life is not doing what you like,
but to like what you are doing."

"Never criticize another person until you walk a mile in their moccasins."

—Harper Lee, *To Kill a Mockingbird*

"Worrying is like sitting in a rocking chair; it passes away time, but doesn't get you anywhere."

Michael McCaffrey

"Go shopping and see how many things you can do without."

"Crossing the bridge before you get to it is like paying the toll twice."

"If you trust in the Lord, you don't worry. If you worry, you don't trust."

—Psalms 37:4

"Blessed is he who expects not,
for he is never disappointed."

"The best way to solve problems is to face them head on."

"If there is no sadness, there is no gladness."

Michael McCaffrey

"Expectation breeds frustration."

"If you didn't have problems,
you wouldn't have to get up in the morning."

"Two men in prison,
one saw bars,
one saw stars."

"Indecision is a sign of weakness of character."

"Be enthusiastic about everything."

"Take care of the needy,
not the greedy."

"The three things that drive all people
are the three P's:
Power, Possessions and Pleasure.
They are all good and useful,
but use them to help others."

"Life is full of miracles,
small and large, but life itself
is a miracle. Enjoy it!"

"Pray, yes, but when you get off your knees, hustle."

"Make things happen,
watch things happen,
wonder what happened."

"Blessed are they who keep
their mouth shut until
they have something to say."

"It is greater to give
than to receive."

—Acts 20:35

"Be charitable to
the uncharitable."

"Kill your enemies
with kindness."

"Arguing with a fool shows
there are two fools."

"Assume everybody is an idiot
and act accordingly."

"A wise man is known,
not so much for the smart things he says,
but for the stupid things he doesn't say."

"An optimist is the person who goes to the horse/dog track with only $2.00."

Michael McCaffrey

"The best way to kill time
is to pray it to death."

Hamlet
Act III, Scene 3
—William Shakespeare

"Eat to live,
not live to eat."

Michael McCaffrey

"You are educated if you can
listen to almost anything
without losing your temper."

"Life is hard enough with the Lord;
I certainly would not
like to try it without him."

"The only thing that happens instantly is when you write a check and hurry to the bank and it beats you."

"I might be crazy,
but I am not stupid."

Michael McCaffrey

"Faith in God;
Trust in yourself."

"If you can't imagine it,
you can't accomplish it."

Michael McCaffrey

"Seek first the kingdom of heaven
and all other things
will be given unto you."

—Luke 12:31
—Matthew 6:33

"Born retired
and had a relapse."

"No one or anything can take away what is in your mind."

"The greatest pleasures
in the world
are in your mind."

"Anytime you think you are indispensable,
take a walk through a cemetery."

"Worry about nothing,
pray about everything,
thank God for anything."

"Think positive, when you wake up
in the morning, say, 'Good morning, God,'
not 'Good God, morning.'
It makes a difference."

"Yes, you will be sick, lose a loved one, have cancer, be broke, or whatever, but rejoice...this too will pass."

—John 14

"The less you say,
the more you say."

"Better late than never."

"Life...live it or lose it."

"Reading a book merely for the words
is like digging a hole
with a fountain pen."

"If you can carry the piano,
you can carry the stool."

"I'd rather owe it to you
than cheat you out of it."

Michael McCaffrey

"The sins you commit 2 by 2,
you pay for 1 by 1."

—Rudyard Kipling 1891

"Don't hold back in life, give everything you have.
It will come back to you multiplied."

—Mark 4:14–20

Michael McCaffrey

"People who say they cannot afford to give, cannot afford not to."

—Mark 12:17

"God made all things good.
Man makes them bad by abuse and excess."

—Romans 8:28

"I know my ultimate home is in heaven,
but I am not homesick yet."

"You can lead a horse to water,
but you cannot make him drink."

—Greek: 11th century

"Don't envy others.
The only person you have to be
better than is yourself."

"Don't worry about money,
as you can't take it with you.
Did you ever see an armored
truck following a hearse?"

Michael McCaffrey

"Live every moment as if it was the last.
One of them will be."